COMMUNICATION
3
A READING SKILLS WORKBOOK FOR ADULTS
FOR TODAY

Program Authors

Linda Ward Beech   Tara McCarthy

STEC   NY

A Division of National Education Corporation

Acknowledgments

Photography:
Jim Myers — cover

Illustrations:
Scott Bieser

ISBN: 0-8114-1927-4

2 3 4 5 6 7 8 9 0 VP 90 89

Table of Contents

Table of Contents

To the Teacher/Tutor

COMMUNICATION FOR TODAY is a reading skills workbook series designed to accompany the textbook series READING FOR TODAY. Each workbook matches each text in:

- strictly controlled vocabulary
- reading level
- phonics and structural skills
- sight vocabulary
- language and comprehension skills

The chart below shows how a typical unit in COMMUNICATION FOR TODAY serves as a follow-up for its matching unit in READING FOR TODAY.

READING FOR TODAY	COMMUNICATION FOR TODAY
Unit Contents	Unit Contents
• Oral language	• Oral language
• Sight words	• Oral reading
• Phonics skills	• Phonics generalizations
• Word structure	• Structural generalizations
• Reading selection	• Extended reading selections
• Comprehension questions	• Comprehension questions
• Life-coping skills	• Writing

Students who use COMMUNICATION FOR TODAY, however, do not simply review, practice, and reinforce oral language skills, phonics skills, sight word recall, and language skills—although there is plenty of that! Students also *extend* the learning they have done. They *read* more good stories with adult themes, written with the strict vocabulary control that puts the reading in their grasp. They *discuss* what they bring of their own experience to the reading they are about to do by responding to purpose-setting questions, thus sharpening their oral-language skills. And they *write*, both to demonstrate comprehension and to respond in their own way to the reading they have done.

COMMUNICATION FOR TODAY is the reading skills program that reviews, practices, reinforces—and *extends!*

Teaching Suggestions

Each unit in COMMUNICATION FOR TODAY follows the pattern outlined below.

Reading and Talking   Page 1

Objectives: To help your student see the connection between reading and talking. To improve comprehension through oral language.

Teaching Steps:
A. Read the question or questions. Encourage your student to talk about the question. Conversation about the question will help your student get ready for the story.
B. Help your student read the story. Remember to praise your student's efforts.
C. Talk about the story. Help your student answer the question. Re-read the story, if necessary.

Reviewing Key Words   Page 2

Objective: To review the sight word vocabulary used in the reading selections. (Every sight word is reviewed at least once.)

Teaching Steps: Be sure your student understands the directions for each exercise. Have student check answers by referring to the back of the book.

Oral Reading   Page 3

Objective: To practice reading word groups (phrases) rather than individual words.

Teaching Steps:
  A. Help your student read and re-read each phrase until each one is smooth and natural. Swing your hand in an arc under each phrase as your pupil reads, to help "push" him or her toward fluency. (A pencil will also suffice.) Praise your student's successes.
  B. Help your student complete the exercise.
  C. Practice reading the entire story for fluency. Re-reading the story after practicing the phrasing will give your student a sense of success.

Phonics Practice   Pages 4 and 5

Objective: To review and reinforce the phonics skills taught in READING FOR TODAY.

Teaching Steps: Be sure your student understands the directions for each exercise. Have student check answers by referring to the back of the book.

Language Skills   Page 6

Objective: To review and reinforce the language skills taught in READING FOR TODAY.

Teaching Steps: Help your student understand the directions for each exercise. Have student check answers by referring to the back of the book.

Comprehension   Page 7

Objectives: To read a story. To answer comprehension questions in writing.

Teaching Steps:
  A. Have your student read the story.
  B. Have the student write the answers to the questions. The following hints will help your student succeed.
     1. The answer to the question may often be found directly stated in the story.
     2. Re-reading the story after reading a question may make it easier to answer the question.
     3. Simply reword the question to answer it in a complete sentence.

Writing and Reading   Page 8

Objectives: To give your student an opportunity to write about his or her own life or life experiences. To reinforce *reading* by writing something for someone else to read.

Teaching Steps:
  A. Encourage your student to get as much on paper as possible. Praise any legitimate attempts to write. Try for more clarity only as your student gains confidence in writing.
  B. When your student is finished writing, you may wish to go back over the writing, following the directions for Part B.

1 Owning a Business

Reading and Talking

A. Talk about it.

Have you worked in a store? Do you have a friend working in one?

B. Read the story.

About My Store

This was my father's music store. Dad mended guitars. I worked for him. I was in the store all the time. I looked at the work he did, and I helped him.

I have my dad's feeling about work. It takes a lot of time to do a job well. I lose some time for play, but that is OK. It works out well for me in the end.

Time went by, and my dad had some trouble with his health. He handed the store to me. The store is not a lot of trouble for me. Yet the store <u>is</u> work. But I'm not going to lose it. I love this old store, trouble and all!

C. Think about it.

Talk about some troubles that go with running a music store.

Reviewing Key Words

A. Read the words in the box. Write the words into the puzzle.

guitar	time	goods
trouble	arrested	top

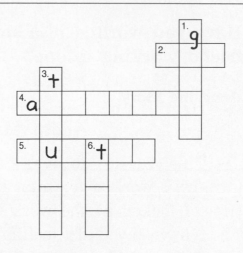

B. Say the words in the box. Write each word next to the word that rhymes with it.

my	don't	top

1. won't   d o n ' t

2. by   __ __

3. mop   __ __ __

C. Use the number code to write the words.

a	b	c	d	e	f	g	h	i	j	k	l	m	n	o
1	2	3	4	5	6	7	8	9	10	11	12	13	14	15

p	q	r	s	t	u	v	w	x	y	z
16	17	18	19	20	21	22	23	24	25	26

13 21 19 9 3   m u s i c   12 15 19 5 __ __ __ __

9 22 5 __ ' __   19 15 13 5 __ __ __ __

Oral Reading

A. Read the phrases in the box aloud. Practice until you can read them smoothly.

---

1. sells tapes and records
2. up and down
3. shoplift some goods
4. sees the guard
5. won't take goods
6. The store sells lots of goods

B. Write the phrases to complete the story.

Lin _sells tapes and records_ in her
₁

store. A man walks _____ by the records.
₂

Will he _____? The
₃

man _____, and the guard sees
₄

him. The man _____ without
₅

paying for them. _____
₆

_____ and loses no money with Kent

on guard.

C. Read the story aloud. Practice until you can read it smoothly.

Phonics: Short e

A. Say the words in the box. They all have the short e sound.

sell	yell	tell	bell	shell
bed	help	sent	met	lend

B. Write other words with the short e sound. Say them.

1. b + end = _bend_

2. l + et = _____

3. t + end = _____

4. f + ell = _____

C. Read each word pair aloud. Circle the word with the short e sound. Write it.

1. (fell)   feel   _fell_

2. eat   end   _____

3. light   let   _____

4. petting   paying   _____

5. seven   she   _____

D. Read each sentence. Circle the word with the short e sound. Write it.

1. Lin will (get) the guard. _get_

2. She uses a bell. _____

3. Kent is the guard. _____

4. The guard fed the dog. _____

5. The dog helps him guard the store. _____

Phonics: Long a

A. Say the words in the box. They all have the long *a* sound.

rake	bake	shake	lake	wake
age	pay	radio	table	they

B. Write other words with the long *a* sound. Say them.

1. t + ake = _____

2. c + ake = _____

3. J + ake = _____

4. f + ake = _____

C. Read each word pair aloud. Circle the word with the long *a* sound. Write it.

1. sake   sad   _____

2. talk   tables   _____

3. age   ad   _____

4. water   wake   _____

5. pan   play   _____

D. Read each sentence. Circle the word with the long *a* sound. Write it.

1. Lin's store sells music, not cakes. _____

2. She has tapes in her store. _____

3. People of all ages use the store. _____

4. One man looked at radios. _____

5. He will pay for one. _____

Phonics: Long a

Compound Words

A. **Write and read the new words.**

1. sun + set = _____

2. hand + out = _____

3. sand + lot = _____

4. pop + gun = _____

5. home + sick = _____

6. bed + time = _____

7. sun + up = _____

B. **Find the two words that make up each word. Write the two words.**

1. someone _____ _____

2. bandstand _____ _____

3. workout _____ _____

4. shoplift _____ _____

5. catwalk _____ _____

6. sundown _____ _____

7. sometimes _____ _____

C. **Read the paragraph. Circle the compound words.**

At (sunset,) someone walked into the store. He was homesick for some country music. We helped him find a good tape. Without a tape he had no music. In the city, a country man likes some old music at bedtime.

Comprehension

A. Read the story.

The Mistake

A workman walked into Lin's store. He had money to buy tapes and records. He looked at all the records by *The Guard Dogs*.

Lin walked up to help him. The store had all the tapes and records by *The Guard Dogs*.

Kent was guarding the store. <u>Guard</u>? <u>Help</u>? Did Lin have to have <u>help</u> from him? Was she in trouble? He ran up to her.

Lin was not in trouble. The man wasn't shoplifting.

Lin laughed. The man was buying records and tapes by *The Guard Dogs*. He did not take them without paying.

The workman laughed. Kent was being a good guard. He was on the job! *The Guard Dogs* is a good band for <u>him</u>!

B. Write the answers to the questions. Use complete sentences.

1. Did the workman look for records and tapes in the store?

   The workman looked for records and tapes in the store.

2. Did Kent run up to Lin?

Writing and Reading

A. **Write your own story. You can use your own idea or find one in the box. You may want to use the phrases below in your story.**

Subjects

Buying	Music	Jobs
buy and sell	hit records	doing a good job
in a store	bands I like	you and the boss
that I see	buying tapes	take a chance
some money down	an up feeling	to make money
to guard money	talk about it	helping people

_____

_____

_____

_____

_____

_____

_____

_____

_____

_____

B. **Read your story. Make any changes you wish. You may want to make it longer. Did you use any compound words? Be sure you spelled them correctly.**

2 Rearing Children

Reading and Talking

A. Talk about it.

Do you have friends who have troubles at home?

B. Read the story.

Running Out

We had troubles at home. My mother ran out on my father. I did not get on with him and his friend Pat. I went to my sister's home in the city.

My sister Jan has a big family, and some of her children got sick. It did not work out for me to be with them. Jan is a good woman, but she had to send me home.

I went — but I did not go to my father's. I had no money, no home, and no job. I was looking for trouble, and I got it!

C. Think about it.

Talk about troubles that children like this can get into.

Reviewing Key Words

A. Look down and across. Find the words in the box and circle them.

brother

children

father

mother

feel

them

find

```
s  x  f  d  w  b  f  w
c  h  i  l  d  r  e  n
t  z  n  h  l  o  e  c
h  n  d  p  m  t  l  p
e  u  m  o  t  h  e  r
m  z  v  a  g  e  m  k
f  a  t  h  e  r  l  o
```

B. Write the words in the box under the letter each begins with.

laugh	age	from	went

a   w

_____   _____

f   l

_____   _____

C. Write the word *time* for each picture.

1. It's _____   2. _____ out!   3. She is on
to get up.

_____.

Oral Reading

A. **Read the phrases in the box aloud. Practice until you can read them smoothly.**

1. A social worker
2. when I was down and out
3. my own parents love me
4. did give me a fine life
5. who have troubles
6. When life is bad for us

B. **Write the phrases to complete the story.**

_____ talked to me about my
1

troubles. She helped me _____
2

_____. She helped me see that _____
3

_____. Both my mother and

father _____
4

at one time. My parents are good people _____
5

_____. _____
6

_____, the social worker helps.

C. **Read the story aloud. Practice until you can read it smoothly.**

Phonics: Short *u*

A. Say the words in the box. They all have the short *u* sound.

up	mug	lug	rug	tug
sun	but	gun	run	us

B. Write other words with the short *u* sound. Say them.

1. b + us = _____

2. h + ug = _____

3. d + ug = _____

4. n + ut = _____

C. Read each word pair aloud. Circle the word with the short *u* sound. Write it.

1. out   up _____

2. bug   big _____

3. gut   go _____

4. buy   bus _____

5. rat   rut _____

D. Read each sentence. Circle the word with the short *u* sound. Write it.

1. Nan had no fun on her own. _____

2. She was nuts to go out on her own. _____

3. She was sick, but no one helped her. _____

4. She is lucky that she met the social

   worker. _____

5. She did not let Nan cut her family

   out. _____

Phonics: Short *u*

Phonics: Long *i*

A. Say the words in the box. They all have the long *i* sound.

vine	wine	dine	mine	shine
find	my	time	five	light

B. Write other words with the long *i* sound. Say them.

1. n + ine = _____

2. l + ife = _____

3. f + ine = _____

4. l + ight = _____

C. Read each word pair aloud. Circle the word with the long *i* sound. Write it.

1. fine   fun   _____

2. pin   pine   _____

3. my   me   _____

4. lake   like   _____

5. lit   light   _____

D. Read each sentence. Circle the word with the long *i* sound. Write it.

1. My mother was feeling sad. _____

2. She got friends to help find me. _____

3. Dad yelled at Jan all the time for sending me home. _____

4. He was mad that I ran out on him. _____

5. I've got troubles to work out. _____

Irregular Plurals

A. Draw a line to match the plural word with its singular form. Write the plural.

1. life
2. man
3. person
4. this
5. woman

a. women _____
b. lives <u>lives</u>
c. these _____
d. men _____
e. people _____

B. Rewrite each sentence so the underlined word or words are singular.

1. The <u>women</u> looked at me.

_____

2. She can help the <u>people</u> with troubles.

_____

3. <u>These</u> <u>men</u> won't help me.

_____

C. Read the paragraph. Circle the plural words.

When I ran out on my sister, I went with a man. This was trouble. Some people are no good, and he was one of them. He had women and children shoplifting for him. My life was bad. This time was bad for me.

Comprehension

A. Read the story.

Don't Do It, Nan

I was mad at my parents. I did not like it when my mother ran out on my dad. I yelled at her to make it work with him, but she did not feel that she had a chance.

My mother did not take me when she went. She had to get a job and set up a home. That is when I went to my sister Jan's. Jan is a good person, but nine people in one home is a lot. I had to go.

My mistake was in not going to my father's home. Being on my own did not help me. It did not help my family. I fell in with a bad group. I got in trouble with the law. I'm lucky that I met the social worker. She is helping my parents and me. Can we be a good family? We'll see!

B. Write the answers to the questions. Use complete sentences.

1. Was Nan mad?

   _____

   _____

2. Did Nan find a good home with her sister Jan?

   _____

   _____

3. Who helped her?

   _____

   _____

Writing and Reading

A. Write your own story. You can use your own idea or find one in the box. You may want to use the phrases below in your story.

Subjects		
Homes	**Troubles**	**Children**
in the city	with parents	all ages
for the holidays	on the job	big hugs
in the country	with friends	lots of love
with the family	work them out	fun to have
to buy	with the law	sick and well

_____

_____

_____

_____

_____

_____

_____

_____

_____

_____

_____

_____

B. Read your story. Did you tell all that you wanted to? Did you write all your plurals correctly? Go back and check.

3 Promoting Health Care

Reading and Talking

A. Talk about it.

When you get sick, who helps you out?

B. Read the story.

Finding Help

Our friend Nell Fine is an old woman. She is in good health, but sometimes she has trouble going to the store for food. My family helps her out. Nell has no family of her own to look in on her and see that she is OK. We stand in for her family.

Sometime Nell will get sick. At that time, we will get help for her from a nurse or a social worker. Friends and family can do a lot, but in times of trouble one has to get help from these people. It's up to them to help a sick person get well.

We have talked to Nell about her health. When she gets sick, these people will help her. She sees that we love her and that makes her feel good.

C. Think about it.

Have you had troubles that friends can not help you with? Tell about these troubles.

Reviewing Key Words

A. Read the words in the box. Read the phrases. Write the correct word after the phrase that tells about it.

social worker	win	group

1. a lot of people _____

2. a helper for people in trouble _____

   _____

3. not lose _____

B. Look down and across. Find the words in the box and circle them. Write them.

smoke

smoking

health

chance

about

a	h	q	s	x	z	h
b	d	s	m	o	k	e
o	z	w	o	j	z	a
u	e	x	k	z	q	l
t	w	i	i	u	e	t
c	h	a	n	c	e	h
r	s	b	g	h	i	j

1. _____

2. _____

3. _____

4. _____

5. _____

C. Use the number code to write these words.

a	b	c	d	e	f	g	h	i	j	k	l	m	n	o
1	2	3	4	5	6	7	8	9	10	11	12	13	14	15

p	q	r	s	t	u	v	w	x	y	z
16	17	18	19	20	21	22	23	24	25	26

2 21 20 _____   20 9 13 5 _____

8 1 19 _____   20 1 12 11 _____

Oral Reading

A. **Read the phrases in the box aloud. Practice until you can read them smoothly.**

1. a doctor at the clinic
2. about my hip problem
3. what the doctor wants
4. more hope of getting well
5. The doctor said
6. when I want to

B. **Write the phrases to complete the story.**

I go to _____.

                                1

We talk _____. I

                                2

do _____. I have

                    3

_____.

                    4

_____ that someday

                    5

I will walk _____ without

                    6

feeling bad. The doctor at the clinic has helped me

with my hip problem.

C. **Read the story aloud. Practice until you can read it smoothly.**

Phonics: Short *i*

A. Say the words in the box. They all have the short *i* sound.

hip	zip	tip	clip	ship
big	him	bin	bit	did

B. Write other words with the short *i* sound. Say them.

1. r + ip = _____

2. d + in = _____

3. s + ip = _____

4. s + ix = _____

C. Read each word pair aloud. Circle the word with the short *i* sound. Write it.

1. fine   fin   _____

2. is   I've   _____

3. fit   find   _____

4. lip   life   _____

5. wine   win   _____

D. Read each sentence. Circle the word with the short *i* sound. Write it.

1. Five people walk to the clinic. _____

2. They sit for a time. _____

3. Ted has a bit of trouble. _____

4. He has a bad hip. _____

5. The doctor will see Ted. _____

Phonics: Long o

A. **Say the words in the box. They all have the long o sound.**

mope	cope	rope	pope
both	home	don't	old

B. **Write other words with the long o sound. Say them.**

1. h + ope = _____

2. g + o = _____

3. sm + oke = _____

4. l + ope = _____

C. **Read each word pair aloud. Circle the word with the long o sound. Write it.**

1. pop   pope _____

2. won't   work _____

3. do   go   _____

4. on   own   _____

5. cop   cope _____

D. **Read each sentence. Circle the word with the long o sound. Write it.**

1. An old woman went to the doctor. _____

2. She had no job. _____

3. She had hope for some help. _____

4. The doctor helped her cope with her problems.

_____

5. The nurse will go with her to shop. _____

Adding -er to Words

A. Add -er. Write the new words. Say them.

1. work + er = _____

2. buy + er = _____

3. rent + er = _____

4. sell + er = _____

5. talk + er = _____

6. help + er = _____

7. walk + er = _____

8. read + er = _____

9. play + er = _____

10. own + er = _____

B. Finish eash sentence with an -er word. Read the sentences.

1. A person who <u>buys</u> is a b_____.

2. A person who <u>helps</u> is a h_____.

3. A person who <u>reads</u> is a r_____.

4. A person who <u>owns</u> is an o_____.

5. A person who <u>plays</u> is a p_____.

C. Write one of the words in each sentence. Read the sentences.

      helper   walker   worker

1. My hip was bad, and I had to use my

  _____.

2. The walker was my _____.

3. The nurse is a _____ at the clinic.

Comprehension

A. Read the story.

A Family in Trouble

Jed Sand was in the clinic today. He was mad at our social worker. She had helped his family find a home. Jed can not find his family.

Jed is not good to Kit and his children. He hits them. He won't give Kit money for food. The woman and the children have got to make a home without him for the time being.

I talked to Jed. He has a big problem. He wants to quit being like he is and be good to his family. Sometimes he gets mad at work. When he gets home, he takes it out on Kit and the children.

Lots of people have a problem like Jed. We have a group at the clinic to help them. Jed will go into this group. He will have to cope with his feelings without yelling at people, and he will not hit his family. I hope that someday Jed can be with his family.

B. Write the answers to the questions. Use complete sentences.

1. Did the social worker help Kit and her children?

_____

_____

2. What is Jed's problem?

_____

_____

Writing and Reading

A. Write your own story. You can use your own idea or find one in the box. You may want to use the phrases below in your story.

Subjects		
Health	**Friends**	**Family**
in good health	have a good time	helping out
feeling well	going out	in the home
a doctor's work	people I like	what children want
at a clinic	feeling social	more work
eat good food	more to do	what I hope for

_____

_____

_____

_____

_____

_____

_____

_____

_____

_____

_____

B. Read your story. Make any changes in it that you wish. You may want to take out some words and use others. Did you add *-er* to mean one who does something? Check your spelling of these words.

4 Overcoming Work Problems

Reading and Talking

A. Talk about it.

When do you have good times and laugh with friends?

B. Read the story.

At the Lot

My friends from work and I play baseball at the sandlot. We forget our problems and have some good laughs.

Tip is our boss when we play. He is a fine player and has helped make us into good players. What is more, we have a winning record. This makes us all feel on top of our lives. We love to play, and we love to win.

The trouble is that Tip is not a good worker on the job. He has problems doing work; he can't cope. The boss at our shop has said that Tip will have to zero in on his work problems and give up playing. What will that do to our chances of winning? You can bet they won't be good without Tip.

C. Think about it.

Talk about times when you have to give up what you like a lot.

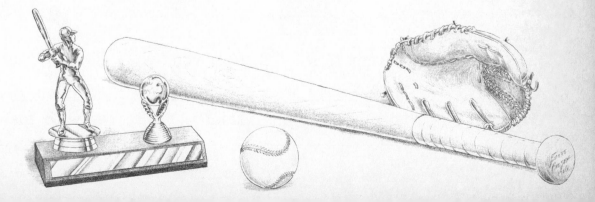

Reviewing Key Words

A. Read the review words.

our	lot	lucky	love
fun	out	friend	

B. Write the words from the box that begin with *l.*

_____ _____ _____

C. Write the words from the box that begin with *o.*

_____ _____

D. Write the words from the box that begin with *f.*

_____ _____

E. Use the number code to write the words.

a b c d e f g h i j k l m n o
1 2 3 4 5 6 7 8 9 10 11 12 13 14 15

p q r s t u v w x y z
16 17 18 19 20 21 22 23 24 25 26

1 12 12 _____   2 15 19 19 _____

7 15 20 _____   14 9 14 5 _____

F. Write the word *play* for each picture.

1. I went to see   2. Can you   3. Will you

a_____.   _____   _____

                   this?   with me?

Oral Reading

A. Read the phrases in the box. Practice until you can read them smoothly.

> 1. of our baseball team
> 2. need him there for the games
> 3. because he can tell us
> 4. does it
> 5. his uniform
> 6. a sad day

B. Write the phrases to complete the story.

Tip is the boss _____ .
                                   1

We _____ .
                           2

He helps us _____
                              3

what is wrong. He _____ in a good way. We
                          4

hope that Tip will not have to give up _____
                                                  5

_____ . That will be _____ for
                                          6

all of us. Maybe Tip and the boss will work out the

problem.

C. Read the story aloud. Practice until you can read it smoothly.

Phonics: Long a

A. Say the words in the box. They all have the long *a* sound.

day	clay	bake	lake	baseball
age	mistake	radio	table	they

B. Write other words with the long a sound. Say them.

1. pl + ay = _____

2. c + ake = _____

3. g + ame = _____

4. f + ake = _____

C. Read each word pair aloud. Circle the word with the long *a* sound. Write it.

1. tape   tip   _____

2. had   hay   _____

3. said   say   _____

4. eight   end   _____

5. that   they   _____

D. Read each sentence. Circle the word with the long *a* sound. Write it.

1. The boss will talk to Tip today. _____

2. We have a game. _____

3. The boss feels the team can play without

   Tip. _____

4. There is no way Tip will like that! _____

5. Will Tip wake up to the problems he has on the

   job? _____

Phonics: Long *e*

A. Say the words in the box. They all have the long *e* sound.

reed	seed	see	reader	heed
eat	we'll	key	he	three

B. Write other words with the long *e* sound. Say them.

1. w + eed = _____

2. f + eel = _____

3. t + eam = _____

4. d + eed = _____

C. Read each word pair aloud. Circle the word with the long *e* sound. Write it.

1. nine   need   _____

2. be   bet   _____

3. she   shell   _____

4. my   me   _____

5. team   ten   _____

D. Read each sentence. Circle the word with the long *e* sound. Write it.

1. Tip was telling me about his problems. _____

2. His boss had talked to him three times about his job. _____

3. Tip had to see someone for help. _____

4. We all talked to Tip. _____

5. A good job is one key to a good life. _____

Recognizing Sentences

**A. Read the sentences and write them below.
Use capital letters where needed.**

boss: don't you like the job?

tip: i like being out in the sun.

_____

_____

_____

_____

**B. Read the sentences and write them below.
Use periods where needed.**

Boss: I see Maybe I can help you
        I need a boss for the men on the van

_____

_____

_____

_____

**C. Read the sentences and write them below.
Use capital letters, exclamation mark, and question
mark correctly.**

tip: that is the job for me
        will you let me have a go at it

_____

_____

_____

_____

Comprehension

A. Read the story.

Tip and the Team

Tip's boss reads people well. He did not let Tip go but helped Tip find a job that was good for him.

Some people like to work in a shop. Some don't. Tip was going nuts. He did not like being in the shop all day. Tip is from the country. He likes to walk in the sun. Because Tip was sad, his work wasn't good. All Tip liked about his job was being with the baseball team.

We hope that a job out of the shop will help Tip do well. He is a fine boss on the team, and he can be a fine boss of the men on the vans. This is a chance for Tip to mend his ways and to feel good about what he does. Doing well on the job is the key to a lot!

B. Write the answers to the questions. Use complete sentences.

1. Did Tip's boss read Tip well?

   _____

   _____

2. What did Tip like about his job?

   _____

   _____

3. Is this job a chance for Tip to mend his ways?

   _____

   _____

Writing and Reading

A. Write your own story. You can use your own idea or find one in the box. You may want to use the phrases below in your story.

Subjects		
Baseball	**Teamwork**	**The Way I Feel**
at work	at home	about me
seeing a game	need for it	about friends
playing it	on the job	being down
in a uniform	give all you have	about winning
win and lose	let us down	talk it out

_____

_____

_____

_____

_____

_____

_____

_____

_____

_____

_____

_____

B. Read your story. Does it say what you want it to? Check your sentences. Do they begin with a capital letter? Do they end with the correct mark? Make the changes you need.

5 Using Prison Time Wisely

Reading and Talking

A. Talk about it.

What do you do when you have time on your hands?

B. Read the story.

Doing Time

The women I see from day to day are about my age. But we're different. They come in after they are arrested. They can't get out because they have to do time. But I can come and go because I work at the prison. I am a guard.

Some of the women don't use time well. They sit and mope. They look for more ways to feel bad about life. Sometimes they make trouble for all of us. But lots of women use time in good ways. They work well at the jobs we give them.

Fay is a woman like that. She has an up feeling about life. She wants a good job when she gets out. When she isn't working, she is reading or talking to her friends.

I have a lot of hope for Fay. She will make it when it's time for her to go.

C. Think about it.

Do you feel that you use time well?

Reviewing Key Words

A. Read the review words.

1. arrested	2. wrong	3. dog
4. mistake	5. his	6. send
7. did	8. fed	9. eat
10. be	11. do	12. law

B. Look at the first six review words. Now look at the box below. Look across and down for the six review words. Circle them and then write them.

l	o	k	n	i	m	r	l
p	i	l	d	h	i	s	w
v	w	e	s	q	s	v	n
a	r	r	e	s	t	e	d
b	o	k	n	i	a	q	o
l	n	a	d	z	k	w	g
r	g	e	v	c	e	o	g

1. _____

2. _____

3. _____

4. _____

5. _____

6. _____

C. Use the number code to write these words.

a	b	c	d	e	f	g	h	i	j	k	l	m	n	o
1	2	3	4	5	6	7	8	9	10	11	12	13	14	15

p	q	r	s	t	u	v	w	x	y	z
16	17	18	19	20	21	22	23	24	25	26

5 1 20 _____   4 9 4 _____

6 5 4 _____   2 5 _____

4 15 _____   12 1 23 _____

Oral Reading

A. Read the phrases in the box aloud. Practice until you can read them smoothly.

> 1. teach the dogs
> 2. will learn different things
> 3. disabled people
> 4. to come, sit, and look out for cars
> 5. the right things to do
> 6. from the prison to June's home

B. Write the phrases to complete the story.

I see Fay _____ we have at
₁

the prison. Sundown _____
₂

_____ from Fay. She will teach him

to help _____. Fay will teach
₃

him _____
₄

_____. June is disabled, but she will

learn _____ for
₅

her dog. In time, Sundown will go _____
₆

_____.

C. Read the story aloud. Practice until you can read it smoothly.

Phonics: Long *i*

A. Say the words in the box. They all have the long *i* sound.

right	night	fight	sight
time	my	by	like

B. Write other words with the long *i* sound. Say them.

1. t + ight = _____

2. l + ight = _____

3. f + ive = _____

C. Read each word pair aloud. Circle the word with the long *i* sound. Write it.

1. I'm   in   _____

2. win   wine   _____

3. fight   fit   _____

4. life   lip   _____

D. Read each sentence. Circle the word with the long *i* sound. Write it.

1. Sundown likes to be with June. _____

2. They are a sight to see! _____

3. It's right for Sundown to go with

   June. _____

4. Fay might see Sundown when she gets

   out. _____

5. Sundown helps June both night and

   day. _____

Phonics: Long *u*

A. Say the words in the box. They all have the long *u* sound.

June	cute	mute
lose	do	you

B. Write other words with the long *u* sound. Say them.

1. d + une = _____

2. f + ood = _____

3. gr + oup = _____

C. Read each word pair aloud. Circle the word with the long *u* sound. Write it.

1. use   us   _____

2. cut   cute   _____

3. group   gun   _____

4. who   won't   _____

D. Read each sentence. Circle the word with the long *u* sound. Write it.

1. June takes Sundown for a walk by the

   lake. _____

2. The dog plays on the dunes. _____

3. Some people say Sundown is cute. _____

4. The woman will use the dog's help going

   home. _____

5. The woman who worked with Sundown did a

   good job. _____

Irregular Verbs

A. Read the sentences. Circle the verbs that show past time.

Present Time	Past Time
1. I do my work.	1. I did my work.
2. The dog is not a pet.	2. The dog was not a pet.
3. We go out.	3. We went out.
4. We take the dogs.	4. We took the dogs.
5. They come with us.	5. They came with us.
6. I give them love.	6. I gave them love.
7. The dogs are fun.	7. The dogs were fun.

B. Read the sentences. Circle the verbs. Write *present* or *past* in the blank.

1. June went to the prison to get a dog. _____

2. She was lucky to get Sundown. _____

3. She took him to her home in the city. _____

4. June gives the dog a lot of love. _____

5. Fay did good work with Sundown. _____

6. Fay and June are friends because of

   Sundown. _____

7. They do like dogs. _____

8. Can Fay come to see Sundown? _____

Comprehension

A. Read the story.

Fay on Her Way!

Today Fay gets out of prison. I have a feeling that she will do well. She is on her way to be with June and Sundown. June will give Fay a home. Fay will stay with June and Sundown and help them. June feels good that she can do something for Fay. She feels that Fay helped <u>her</u> in a big way by teaching Sundown.

Fay wants to work with disabled people. She will learn about them by being with June from day to day. The social worker is going to find a job for Fay in a city clinic. Lots of people with troubles and problems go to a clinic. Fay will make them feel good. She will give them hope. Fay is like that. She has a way about her. She makes friends, and people like her.

Fay is on her way to the fine things in life. She may make mistakes. We all do. But they won't be the kind of mistakes that get a person into prison!

B. Write the answers to the questions. Use complete sentences.

1. Is Fay going to work?

_____

_____

2. Does June want to do something for Fay?

_____

_____

Writing and Reading

A. Write your own story. You can use your own idea or find one in the box. You may want to use the phrases below in your story.

Subjects		
Uses Time Well	**Prisons**	**Pets**
learning things	feel down and out	something to love
helping people	seeing the family	to feed a pet
went to the city	in a big group	a dog and a cat
playing music	on radio and TV	a lot of money
friends and family	learning a job	going for a walk

_____

_____

_____

_____

_____

_____

_____

_____

_____

B. Read your story. What can you add? What can you take out? Look for words that show past time. Did you spell them correctly? Draw a line under words you want to look up and check.

6 Job Satisfaction

Reading and Talking

A. Talk about it.

What are your feelings about people in uniforms?

B. Read the story.

A Job To Do

My job is with the law. A lot of people get out of my way because I'm a cop. They don't like to be stopped for running a light and things like that. To them, a woman in uniform is trouble!

But I see things in a different way. People in cars need the laws and the cops who give out tickets. We all need them.

Cops do a lot of things for people on the go. I stop and help people in disabled cars. I help people when they lose the way. I do what I have to do. I make arrests. I see that people who need to, get to a doctor. I stand for the law, but I'm a friend to people on the go.

C. Think about it.

Talk about the laws that are needed for people who drive cars.

Reviewing Key Words

A. Read the words in the box. Read the phrases. Write the correct word after the phrase that tells about it.

fit	son	job	bet

1. the work one does _____

2. take a chance _____

3. feeling healthy _____

4. one of parents' children _____

B. First write the words that begin with vowels. Then write the words that begin with consonants.

on	read	make	no
holiday	hand	son	old

1. _____ _____

2. _____ _____

_____ _____

_____ _____

C. Write the word *will* for each picture. Use a capital letter to begin a sentence or a name.

1. _____ you dine with me?

2. She is reading the _____.

3. _____ is my friend.

Oral Reading

A. **Read the phrases in the box aloud. Practice until you can read them smoothly.**

> 1. hot days and cold nights
> 2. on the road
> 3. drive well and mind the laws
> 4. to stop heavy rigs
> 5. trucks carry
> 6. lonely to work

B. **Write the phrases to complete the story.**

On both _____,
$\quad\quad\quad\quad\quad\quad\quad\quad\quad$ 1

a cop like me is _____. I see
$\quad\quad\quad\quad\quad\quad\quad$ 2

that people _____
$\quad\quad\quad\quad\quad\quad\quad\quad\quad$ 3

_____. Sometimes I have _____
$\quad\quad\quad\quad\quad\quad\quad\quad\quad\quad$ 4

_____. Some _____ a
$\quad\quad\quad\quad\quad\quad\quad\quad$ 5

lot of heavy goods. There are laws about what a

truck can carry.

Is it _____ on the road
$\quad\quad\quad\quad\quad\quad$ 6

all the time? No! I love it!

C. **Read the story aloud. Practice until you can read it smoothly.**

Phonics: Short *i*

A. Say the words in the box. They all have the short *i* sound.

dig	lip	into	clinic	shoplift
fit	bin	sister	sick	zipper

B. Write other words with the short *i* sound. Say them.

1. f + ig = _____

2. k + in = _____

3. h + ip = _____

4. p + ig = _____

C. Read each word pair aloud. Circle the word with the short *i* sound. Write it.

1. din   dine _____

2. fight   fit _____

3. will   well _____

4. gave   give _____

5. big   bat _____

D. Read each sentence. Circle the word with the short *i* sound. Write it.

1. A lot of truckers carry goods to the city. _____

2. When I see a disabled truck, I stop to help. _____

3. This can take time. _____

4. I helped dig a truck out of the sand. _____

5. I have helped sick people get to a doctor. _____

Phonics: Long *o*

A. Say the words in the box. They all have the long *o* sound.

fold	gold	lonely	pope	social worker
smoke	old	both	home	zero

B. Write other words with the long *o* sound. Say them.

1. h + old = _____

2. s + old = _____

3. m + ope = _____

4. t + old = _____

C. Read each word pair aloud. Circle the word with the long *o* sound. Write it.

1. hope   hop   _____

2. don't   do   _____

3. no   not   _____

4. bed   bold   _____

5. rip   rope   _____

D. Read each sentence. Circle the word with the long *o* sound. Write it.

1. Sometimes I go to work at night. _____

2. I use my radio a lot. _____

3. On cold nights I take some hot food

   with me. _____

4. My boss told me that I may have to work on

   some holidays. _____

5. Some holidays I want to be home with my

   family. _____

Dropping Final -e To Add -ed and -ing

A. Drop the final -e. Add -ed. Then add -ing.

	-ed	-ing
1. hope	hoped	hoping
2. tape	_____	_____
3. age	_____	_____
4. shine	_____	_____
5. use	_____	_____
6. love	_____	_____

B. Read the sentences. Circle the words that end in -ed and -ing. Write them.

1. I like driving in the city. _____

2. I get my radio tuned in right. _____

3. I used to like smoking in the car,

   but I gave it up. _____ _____

4. I am using my time in different ways. _____

C. Write one of these words in each sentence.

loved	taped	hoped	giving	waking

1. I have _____ cars all my life.

2. I _____ to get a job like this.

3. This job is _____ me lots of chances
   to see the city.

4. I don't like _____ up at five.

5. Sometimes I play _____ music in
   my car.

Comprehension

A. Read the story.

On the Road

I wanted to go on the road because I love driving. But my family needed me at home. They did not want me to be on the road for days at a time. Being a cop is a good way to do some driving and yet be home some of the time.

I work some nights, some days, and some holidays. But I get lots of time at home. My pay isn't bad, and I have the right to use the clinic when I'm sick.

I have learned a lot about people in my job. Some people are different when they get in a car. They drive like they own the road. They want to fight me when I stop them. I have learned to tune out bad talk. I don't want trouble. I want to see that people carry out the driving laws.

B. Write the answers to the questions. Use complete sentences.

1. What did this person want to do for a job?

   _____

   _____

2. When does she work?

   _____

   _____

3. What are *some* people like when they get in a car?

   _____

   _____

Writing and Reading

A. Write your own story. You can use your own idea or find one in the box. You may want to use the phrases below in your story.

Subjects		
Driving	**Working at Night**	**Learning About People**
on the road	being a cop	good and bad
in a truck	mopping up	helping out
a fine car	at a clinic	teaching children
within laws	a good guard	what they are like
heavy rigs	lonely job	loving and learning

_____

_____

_____

_____

_____

_____

_____

_____

_____

B. Read your story. Did it come out the way you thought it would? Make changes to improve it. Check the words to which you added -ed and -ing. Did you drop the e in the right places?

7 Working in the Performing Arts

Reading and Talking

A. Talk about it.

What job do you want? Tell what you like about that job.

B. Read the story.

Looking for Something Good

My friends and I talk a lot about jobs and money. We want jobs that are fun to do, but we want these jobs to pay well. You have to look a lot to find a job that does these two things!

I feel you have to find a job that fits the person you are. Take me. I like to work on my own. I work well without a boss telling me what to do all the time. I can't work well when people are talking near me.

My friends Ted and Will are different from me. They like to work with people. They love the feeling of being in a big group of workers.

I'm going to learn all I can and read all I can. I'll find the right job for me. And Will and Ted will find what is right for them.

C. Think about it.

Do you like to work in a group?

Reviewing Key Words

A. **Circle the words in the box that have long vowel sounds.**

come	day	road	want
see	truck	hope	life

B. **Draw a line to match each word and its opposite.**

1. down   a. different

2. there   b. not there

3. day   c. give

4. alike   d. up

5. take   e. night

C. **Write the word *down* for each picture.**

1. Ed fell

_____.

2. Kay feels

_____.

3. This has

_____ in it.

Oral Reading

A. **Read the phrases in the box aloud. Practice until you can read them smoothly.**

> 1. a movie about city streets
> 2. parts in the movie
> 3. to see many big stars
> 4. by the camera together
> 5. a heavy bag
> 6. to get seats at the movie

B. **Write the phrases to complete the story.**

Some people are making _____
_____. Ted and Will feel lucky

to have _____. They

get _____. Ted

and the big star walk _____

_____. Will's part is to carry _____

_____ for the star. My friends and I

will stand in line _____

_____ when it comes out.

C. **Read the story aloud. Practice until you can read it smoothly.**

Phonics: Short *a*

A. Say the words in the box. They all have the short *a* sound.

lag	tag	bandstand	camera	wag
bad	mat	sand	an	at

B. Write other words with the short *a* sound. Say them.

1. n + ag = _____

2. f + an = _____

3. c + at = _____

4. r + ag = _____

C. Read each word pair aloud. Circle the word with the short *a* sound. Write it.

1. mad   make   _____

2. say   sag   _____

3. rug   rag   _____

4. pat   pet   _____

5. gag   gig   _____

D. Read each sentence. Circle the word with the short *a* sound. Write it.

1. I might like a chance to be in a

   movie. _____

2. You have to learn what you do well. _____

3. My sister has a job she does not like. _____

4. She works at a store. _____

5. She might like working with

   cameras. _____

Phonics: Long *e*

A. Say the words in the box. They all have the long *e* sound.

wheat	meat	deed	movie	team
feel	we'll	he	she	three

B. Write other words with the long *e* sound. Say them.

1. b + eat = _____

2. n + eed = _____

3. s + eat = _____

4. r + eed = _____

C. Read each word pair aloud. Circle the word with the long *e* sound. Write it.

1. neat   net   _____

2. fed   feel   _____

3. ten   treat   _____

4. seed   sell   _____

5. time   team   _____

D. Read each sentence. Circle the word with the long *e* sound. Write it.

1. My sister May is a big reader. _____

2. May likes to be on her own. _____

3. I like working with lots of different

   people. _____

4. I loved my job on the street. _____

5. I got to see what was going on! _____

Writing Quotations

A. Read the sentences. Circle the quotation marks. Underline the words that are not spoken.

1. Nell said, "Being in movies is not for me. I like to work on the land."

2. "We all want different jobs," said Will.

3. "It's a good thing," said Nell, "that there are lots of different jobs."

B. Write each sentence below. Add quotation marks, commas, and question marks.

1. A job playing baseball is OK with me laughed Ted.

   "A job playing baseball is OK with me," laughed Ted.

2. June said I want to work with the disabled.

   _____

   _____

3. Will you learn to be a social worker said Ted.

   _____

   _____

4. I like being in the movies Will said.

   _____

   _____

5. Jan said I like working in the country. No city jobs for me!

   _____

   _____

Comprehension

A. Read the story.

Working in a Group

When you go to a movie, you see the stars, and that is about it. You don't see all the people who worked to make the movie a hit. You don't see the people who worked the cameras and the lights. You don't see the people who had to carry things up and down the movie set. But without people like these, there is no movie at all. These people are a big part of the movie group.

It's like that with a big band. You see the people making music, and you hop up and down and yell for them. But the ones who make music can't do it without the people who help them. There are people who make the lights right, carry in the guitars, set up the seats, take tickets, and get things going on time.

A lot of work can go into making a big movie and a hit band. Many people find work helping with movies and bands. Stars can't be stars at all without these people to help them.

B. Write the answers to the questions. Use complete sentences.

1. What work is there to do with a hit band?

_____

_____

2. Can a star be a star without help?

_____

_____

Writing and Reading

A. Write your own story. You can use your own idea or find one in the box. You might want to use the phrases below in your story.

Subjects		
Having Fun	**Getting a Job**	**Learning To Read**
at the movies	talk to someone	something I want
a good band	the job I want	to read to my
without TV	find out what	children
laughing with	to do	reading on the job
friends	not many jobs	teachers of reading
go out to eat	taking a chance	read on my own

_____

_____

_____

_____

_____

_____

_____

_____

_____

_____

B. Read your story. Did you use your best ideas? Do you want to add more? In your story, did you use words that people say? Did you use quotation marks, commas, and capital letters in the right way? Check your story.

Answer Key

Unit 1

page 2 **A. 1.** goods **2.** top **3.** trouble **4.** arrested **5.** guitar **6.** time **B. 2.** my **3.** top **C.** lose, I've, some

page 3 **B. 2.** up and down **3.** shoplift some goods **4.** sees the guard **5.** won't take goods **6.** The store sells lots of goods

page 4 **B. 2.** let **3.** tend **4.** fell **C. 2.** end **3.** let **4.** petting **5.** seven **D. 2.** bell **3.** Kent **4.** fed **5.** helps

page 5 **B. 1.** take **2.** cake **3.** Jake **4.** fake **C. 1.** sake **2.** tables **3.** age **4.** wake **5.** play **D. 1.** cakes **2.** tapes **3.** ages **4.** radios **5.** pay

page 6 **A. 2.** handout **3.** sandlot **4.** popgun **5.** homesick **6.** bedtime **7** sunup **B. 2.** band, stand **3.** work, out **4.** shop, lift **5.** cat, walk **6.** sun, down **7.** some, times **C.** sunset, someone, into, homesick, without, bedtime

page 7 **B. 2.** Kent ran to help Lin.

Unit 2

page 10 **A.** These words should be circled: mother, father, find, feel, them **B. 2.** went **3.** from **4.** laugh **C. 1.** time **2.** time **3.** time

page 11 **B. 1.** A social worker **2.** when I was down and out **3.** my own parents love me **4.** did give me a fine life **5.** who have troubles **6.** When life is bad for us

page 12 **B. 1.** bus **2.** hug **3.** dug **4.** nut **C. 1.** up **2.** bug **3.** gut **4.** bus **5.** rut **D. 1.** fun **2.** nuts **3.** but **4.** lucky **5.** cut

page 13 **B. 1.** nine **2.** life **3.** fine **4.** light **C. 1.** fine **2.** pine **3.** my **4.** like **5.** light **D. 1.** My **2.** find **3.** time **4.** I **5.** I've

page 14 **A. 2.** d, men **3.** e, people **4.** c, these **5.** a, women **B. 2.** She can help the person with troubles. **3.** This man won't help me. **C.** people, women, children

page 15 **B. 1.** Nan was mad at her parents.

2. Nan did not find a good home with Jan. **3.** The social worker helped Nan.

Unit 3

page 18 **A. 1.** group **2.** social worker **3.** win **B.** (order may vary) **1.** smoke **2.** health **3.** about **4.** chance **5.** smoking **C.** but, time, has, talk

page 19 **B. 1.** a doctor at the clinic **2.** about my hip problem **3.** what the doctor wants **4.** more hope of getting well **5.** The doctor said **6.** when I want to

page 20 **B. 1.** rip **2.** din **3.** sip **4.** six **C. 1.** fin **2.** is **3.** fit **4.** lip **5.** win **D. 1.** clinic **2.** sit **3.** bit **4.** hip **5.** will

page 21 **B. 1.** hope **2.** go **3.** smoke **4.** lope **C. 1.** pope **2.** won't **3.** go **4.** own **5.** cope **D. 1.** old **2.** no **3.** hope **4.** cope **5.** go

page 22 **A. 1.** worker **2.** buyer **3.** renter **4.** seller **5.** talker **6.** helper **7.** walker **8.** reader **9.** player **10.** owner **B. 1.** buyer **2.** helper **3.** reader **4.** owner **5.** player **C. 1.** walker **2.** helper **3.** worker

page 23 **B. 1.** The social worker helped Kit and the children by finding them a home. **2.** Jed hits his family and yells at them.

Unit 4

page 26 **B.** lot, lucky, love **C.** our, out **D.** friend, fun **E.** all, boss, got, nine **F. 1.** play **2.** play **3.** play

page 27 **B. 1.** of our baseball team **2.** need him there for the games **3.** because he can tell us **4.** does it **5.** his uniform **6.** a sad day

page 28 **B. 1.** play **2.** cake **3.** game **4.** fake **C. 1.** tape **2.** hay **3.** say **4.** eight **5.** they **D. 1.** today **2.** game **3.** play **4.** way **5.** wake

page 29 **B. 1.** weed **2.** feel **3** team **4.** deed **C. 1.** need **2.** be **3.** she **4.** me **5.** team **D. 1.** me **2.** three **3.** see **4.** We **5.** key

page 30 **A.** Boss: Don't you like the job? Tip: I like being out in the sun. **B.** I see. Maybe I can help you. I need a boss for the men on the van. **C.** That is the job for me! Will you let me have a go at it?

page 31 **B. 1.** Tip's boss reads him well. **2.** Tip likes being with the team. **3.** This job is a chance for Tip to mend his ways.

Unit 5

page 34 **B.** (order may vary) his, wrong, send, arrested, mistake, dog **C. 1.** eat **2.** did **3.** fed **4.** be **5.** do **6.** law

page 35 **B. 1.** teach the dogs **2.** will learn different things **3.** disabled people **4.** to come, sit, and look out for cars **5.** the right things to do **6** from the prison to June's home

page 36 **B. 1.** tight **2.** light **3.** five **C. 1.** I'm **2.** wine **3.** fight **4.** life **D. 1.** likes **2.** sight **3.** right **4.** might **5.** night

page 37 **B. 1.** dune **2.** food **3.** group **C. 1.** use **2.** cute **3.** group **4.** who **D. 1.** June **2.** dunes **3.** cute **4.** use **5.** who

page 38 **A. 1.** did **2.** was **3.** went **4.** took **5.** came **6.** gave **7.** were **B. 1.** went, past **2.** was, past **3.** took, past **4.** gives, present **5.** did, past **6.** are, present **7.** do, present **8.** come, present

page 39 **B. 1.** Fay is going to work at a clinic. **2.** June wants to help Fay because Fay worked with Sundown.

Unit 6

page 42 **A. 1.** job **2.** bet **3.** fit **4.** son **B. 1.** on, old **2.** read, make, holiday, no, hand, sun **C. 1.** will **2.** will **3.** Will

page 43 **B. 1.** hot days and cold nights **2.** on the road **3.** drive well and mind the laws **4.** to stop heavy rigs **5.** trucks carry **6.** lonely to work

page 44 **B. 1.** fig **2.** kin **3.** hip **4.** pig **C. 1.** din **2.** fit **3.** will **4.** give **5.** big **D. 1.** city **2.**

disabled **3.** This **4.** dig **5.** sick

page 45 **B. 1.** hold **2.** sold **3.** mope **4.** told **C. 1.** hope **2.** don't **3.** no **4.** bold **5.** rope **D. 1.** go **2.** radio **3.** cold **4.** told **5.** home

page 46 **A. 1.** hoped, hoping **2.** taped, taping **3.** aged, aging **4.** shined, shining **5.** used, using **6.** loved, loving **B. 1.** driving **2.** tuned **3.** used, smoking **4.** using **C. 1.** loved **2.** hoped **3.** giving **4.** waking **5.** taped

page 47 **B. 1.** She wanted to go on the road as a driver. **2.** She works some nights, some days, and some holidays. **3.** Some people are different.

Unit 7

page 50 **A.** day, road, see, hope, life **B. 1.** up **2.** not there **3.** night **4.** different **5.** give **C.1.** down **2.** down **3.** down

page 51 **1.** a movie about city streets **2.** parts in the movie **3.** to see many big stars **4.** by the camera together **5.** a heavy bag **6.** to get seats at the movie

page 52 **B. 1.** nag **2.** fan **3.** cat **4.** rag **C.1.** mad **2.** sag **3.** rag **4.** pat **5.** gag **D. 1.** chance **2.** have **3.** has **4.** at **5.** cameras

page 53 **B. 1.** beat **2.** need **3.** seat **4.** reed **C. 1.** neat **2.** feel **3.** treat **4.** seed **5.** team **D. 1.** reader **2.** be **3.** people **4.** street **5.** see

page 54 **A. 1.** <u>Nell said</u>, "Being in movies is not for me. I like to work on the land." **2.** "We all want different jobs," <u>said Will</u>. **3.** "It's a good thing," <u>said Nell</u>, "that there are lots of different jobs." **B. 1.** "A job playing baseball is OK with me," laughed Ted. **2.** June said, "I want to work with the disabled." **3.** "Will you learn to be a social worker?" said Ted. **4.** "I like being in the movies," Will said. **5.** Jan said, "I like working in the country. No city jobs for me!"

page 55 **1.** There are people who work with lights, carry in guitars, set up seats, take tickets, and get things going on time for a band. **2.** No. A star cannot be a star without help.